HOW ARE THEY **DIFFERENT?**

Tell Me the DIFFERENCE Between a

FROG and a TOAD

Leigh Rockwood

PowerKiDS press

New York

Published in 2013 by The Rosen Publishing Group, Inc.
29 East 21st Street, New York, NY 10010

First Edition

Editor: Joanne Randolph
Book Design: Kate Laczynski

Library of Congress Cataloging-in-Publication Data

Rockwood, Leigh.
 Tell me the difference between a frog and a toad / by Leigh Rockwood. — 1st ed.
    p. cm. — (How are they different?)
 Includes index.
 ISBN 978-1-4488-9636-3 (library binding) — ISBN 978-1-4488-9730-8 (pbk.) — ISBN 978-1-4488-9731-5 (6-pack)
 1. Frogs—Juvenile literature. 2. Toads—Juvenile literature. I. Title.
 QL668.E2R544 2013
 597.8'9—dc23
                    2012020317

Manufactured in the United States of America

CPSIA Compliance Information: Batch #W13PK5 : For Further Information contact Rosen Publishing, New York, New York at 1-800-237-9932

CONTENTS

Frogs and toads are **amphibians** that belong to a scientific order, or grouping, called Anura. This is the most widespread order of amphibians. There are around 4,000 **species** of amphibians in this order.

Because they belong to the same order, frogs and toads have many

Frogs and toads, like all amphibians, begin life in the water. Frogs, such as this one, tend to stay close to water as adults, while toads spend most of their time on dry land.

Toads generally have lumpy skin. Because of this, some people think toads can give you warts. This is not true, though.

things in common. These similarities can make it hard to tell the difference between a toad and a frog. Some frogs even have the word "toad" in their common names! This book will teach you more about frogs and toads, including how to tell these amphibians apart.

TRUE FROGS, TRUE TOADS

When you hear the word "frog" or "toad," the animals that you think of are likely what scientists call true frogs and true toads. "True" means that the animal fits within the scientific classification of what a frog or a toad is.

Tree frogs, such as this red-eyed tree frog, are not part of the true frog family. They are smaller than true frogs and have sticky toe pads to let them climb trees.

American toads are true toads. They can be found throughout much of the eastern United States and Canada.

True frogs belong to the Ranidae family, which has about 600 species in it. Bullfrogs, wood frogs, and leopard frogs are true frogs. True toads belong to the Bufonidae family, which has about 350 species in it. American toads, green toads, and Great Plains toads are true toads. Tree frogs and spadefoot toads are two examples of frogs and toads that are not true frogs and toads.

HOW ARE FROGS AND TOADS ALIKE?

Frogs and toads have lots of things in common. Both of these animals begin their lives in the water and breathe with gills. As they mature into adulthood, frogs and toads breathe air with their lungs and live on land. This amazing change frogs and toads undergo is called a **metamorphosis**. The name "amphibian" means "two lives" and refers to the change these animals undergo in their lives.

Frogs' and toads' bodies are similar, too. Known to be excellent jumpers, their hind legs are longer than their front legs. They also have squat bodies with short backbones.

Here you can see the long back legs and the much shorter front legs on this frog. The long legs are made for jumping. In fact, some frogs can jump more than 10 or 20 times their body length.

9

This bullfrog rests on a lily pad. It can quickly jump into the water if it senses danger or if its skin is drying out.

One way to tell a frog from a toad is to take a closer look at the animal's skin. Frogs have smooth, moist skin. They can take in water and oxygen through this moist skin. To keep their skin from drying out, frogs are more likely to live close to water.

10

Toads can live farther away from water than frogs can. This is because they have thicker, dry skin. Their skin is also often warty, or bumpy. Toads also have special glands near each eye. These glands let out a poison that keeps many **predators** from eating the toad.

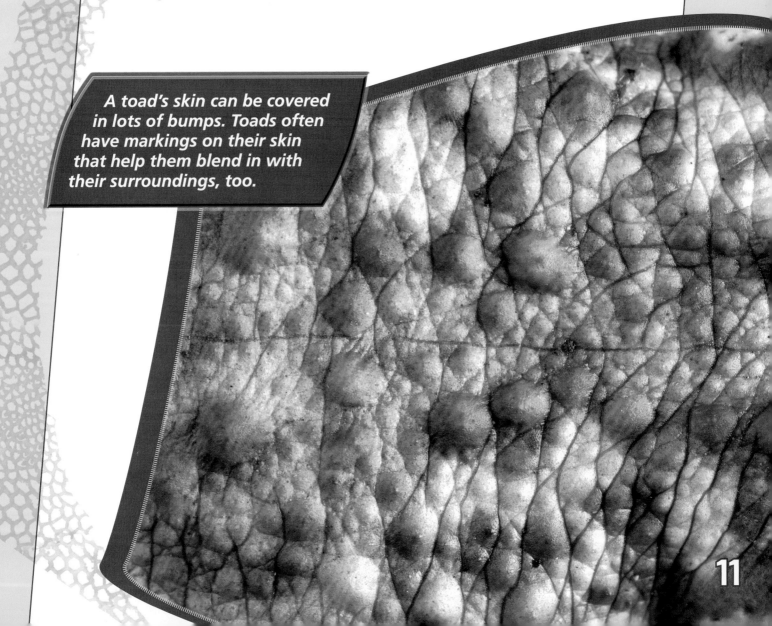

A toad's skin can be covered in lots of bumps. Toads often have markings on their skin that help them blend in with their surroundings, too.

COMPARING FROGS

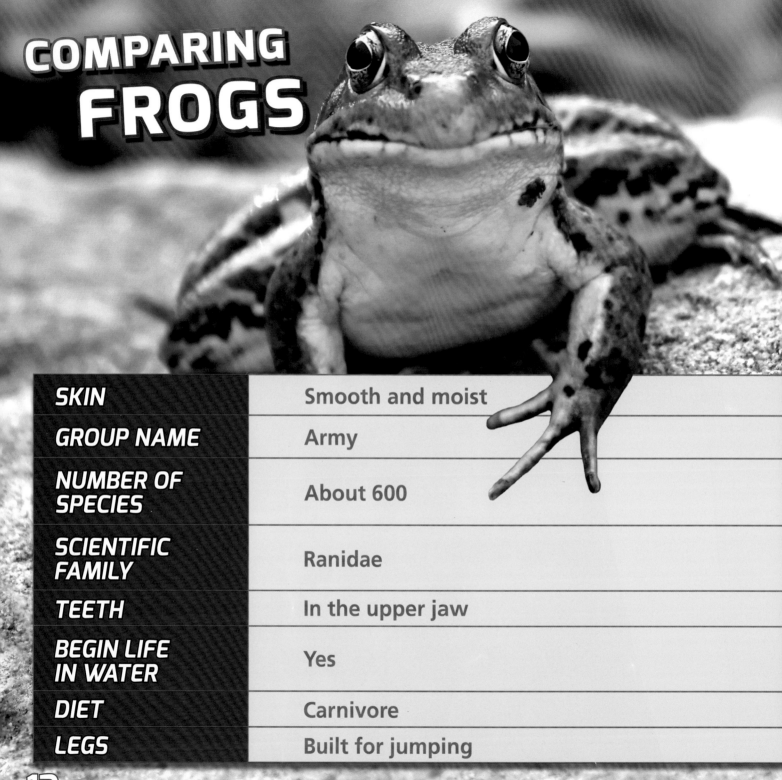

SKIN	Smooth and moist
GROUP NAME	Army
NUMBER OF SPECIES	About 600
SCIENTIFIC FAMILY	Ranidae
TEETH	In the upper jaw
BEGIN LIFE IN WATER	Yes
DIET	Carnivore
LEGS	Built for jumping

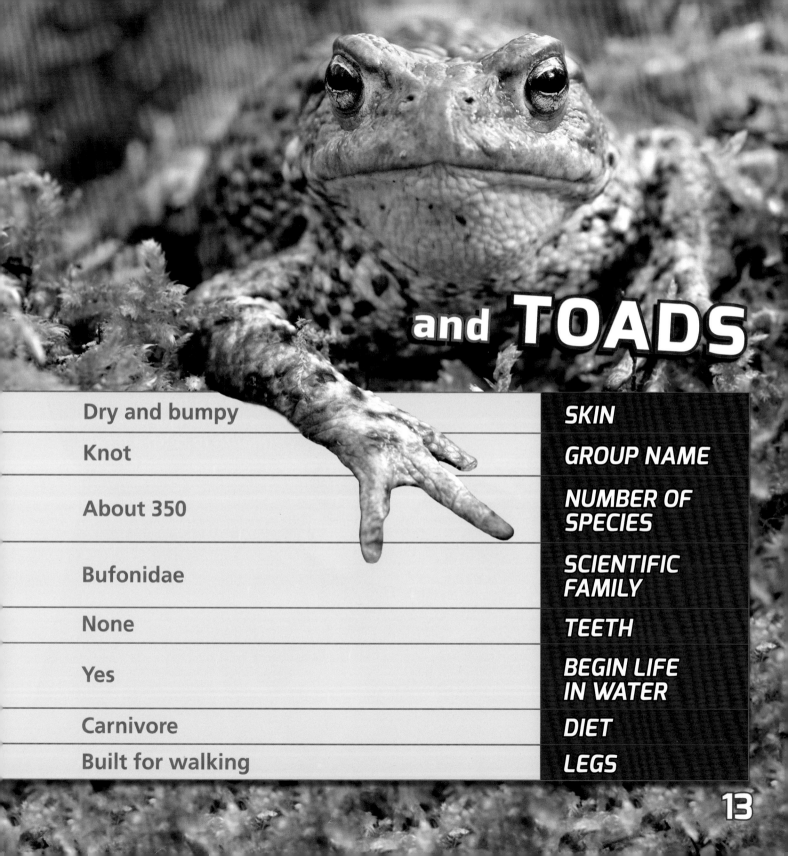

and **TOADS**

Dry and bumpy	*SKIN*
Knot	*GROUP NAME*
About 350	*NUMBER OF SPECIES*
Bufonidae	*SCIENTIFIC FAMILY*
None	*TEETH*
Yes	*BEGIN LIFE IN WATER*
Carnivore	*DIET*
Built for walking	*LEGS*

WHAT'S FOR DINNER?

Frogs and toads have a similar diet. They eat insects, worms, slugs, and spiders. Larger frogs and toads also eat mice and other small animals. In Australia, the cane toad is an **invasive** species that is known for eating pet food from bowls that have been left outside!

Here a toad shoots its sticky tongue out of its mouth to catch a meal.

Frogs and toads eat many kinds of insects. This frog is enjoying a grasshopper for its lunch.

Frogs and toads use their eyesight to sense moving **prey**. Then, with a flick of its long, sticky tongue, the frog or toad captures its dinner and swallows it. Frogs have weak teeth in their upper jaws that they can use to hold on to or crush food if they need to, but toads do not.

LOOK AT THE LEGS

Another place you can find differences between frogs and toads is their legs. Frogs have long, powerful hind legs that are built for jumping. They can jump as much as 20 times the length of their bodies! Most true frogs have webbed feet. These help the frog move through the water better.

This frog is leaping into the air with its long back legs. As you can see, this frog's back legs are longer than its body is.

Toads can jump, but they do not jump as far as frogs. They use their back legs to walk along the ground. You can see that this toad has partly webbed back feet.

Here you can see the frog's webbed back feet as it floats in the water. Webbed feet help animals move quickly through the water.

Toads have shorter legs and move by walking with the occasional short hop. Depending on the species, a true toad's feet may be slightly webbed or they may have completely separated toes.

HOME, SWEET HOME

Frogs are native to every continent except for Antarctica. They live in **habitats** that are near ponds and lakes or other bodies of freshwater. Toads are native to every continent except Antarctica and Australia. They live in a wider range of habitats than frogs, from forests to grasslands and even some deserts!

Left: Toads live in many kinds of habitats. This toad rests in a mossy hollow in a forest. Below: Frogs are often found in or near ponds, lakes, and swamps.

The Fowler's toad lives in floodplains, near rivers, and on the edges of woodlands in Florida. It digs burrows in sandy places in which it can hide during the day.

Frogs and toads are **cold-blooded**, meaning that their body temperature is the same as the temperature of their surroundings. Species that live where it gets cold become dormant, or inactive, during the winter in order to **survive**. They will burrow into the ground and stay there until the weather gets warm again in the spring.

BABY FROGS AND TOADS

As do all amphibians, frogs and toads **mate** and lay their eggs in the water. Female frogs tend to lay their eggs in clusters, while female toads generally lay eggs in chainlike formations. When the eggs hatch, the babies, or tadpoles, look like fish that are made of heads and tails.

Frogs and toads lay their eggs in water. Do you see the jellylike eggs with the dark centers here?

At first, tadpoles look like tiny fish, but over time they start to grow legs.

As baby frogs and toads grow, they may leave the water for short periods. They still have tails at this stage. This froglet will soon lose its tail completely and become a full-grown frog.

As the tadpole goes through its metamorphosis, it begins to grow legs. The rest of its body absorbs the tail. The tadpole develops lungs and loses its gills. All of the changes that turn a tadpole into a frog or toad take place over just three to four months.

The next time you visit a zoo, go to the amphibian house so you can look at different toads and frogs up close. Do you now know how to tell the difference?

Many frogs and toads are plentiful. Others, like the California red-legged

Frogs and toads can be easily hurt by environmental and climate changes. We need to take care of our planet to keep frogs and toads safe.

frog, are in trouble. The scientists who study amphibians help us learn about how to keep frog and toad populations balanced so these animals will continue to thrive.

GLOSSARY

amphibians (am-FIH-bee-unz) Animals that spend the first part of their lives in water and the rest on land.

cold-blooded (KOHLD-bluh-did) Having body heat that changes with the heat around the body.

habitats (HA-buh-tats) The surroundings where animals or plants naturally live.

invasive (in-VAY-siv) Taking over an ecosystem in a way that hurts native plants and animals.

mate (MAYT) To come together to make babies.

metamorphosis (meh-tuh-MOR-fuh-sus) A complete change in form.

predators (PREH-duh-terz) Animals that kill other animals for food.

prey (PRAY) An animal that is hunted by another animal for food.

species (SPEE-sheez) One kind of living thing. All people are one species.

survive (sur-VYV) To continue to exist or stay alive.

INDEX

WEBSITES

Due to the changing nature of Internet links, PowerKids Press has developed an online list of websites related to the subject of this book. This site is updated regularly. Please use this link to access the list: www.powerkidslinks.com/hatd/frto/